SUPER CHEF

The Cooking of
ITALY

For my mother, Virginia Mary Locricchio,
who taught me that anything was possible.

This author's sincere gratitude to Peter Mavrikis, Michelle Bisson, Kay Petronio, and Anahid Hamparian.

Published by Marshall Cavendish Benchmark
An imprint of Marshall Cavendish Corporation
All rights reserved.

Website: www.marshallcavendish.us

Text © 2012 by Matthew Locricchio

Food photographs © 2012 Jack McConnell, McConnell, McNamara & Company
Map © 2012 by Mike Reagan
Illustrations by Janet Hamlin
Illustrations © 2012 by Marshall Cavendish Corporation

This publication represents the opinions and views of the author based on Matthew Locricchio's personal experience, knowledge, and research. The information in this book serves as a general guide only. The author and publisher have used their best efforts in preparing this book and disclaim liability rising directly and indirectly from the use and application of this book.

Other Marshall Cavendish Offices:
Marshall Cavendish International (Asia) Private Limited, 1 New Industrial Road, Singapore 536196 • Marshall Cavendish International (Thailand) Co Ltd. 253 Asoke, 12th Flr, Sukhumvit 21 Road, Klongtoey Nua, Wattana, Bangkok 10110, Thailand • Marshall Cavendish (Malaysia) Sdn Bhd, Times Subang, Lot 46, Subang Hi-Tech Industrial Park, Batu Tiga, 40000 Shah Alam, Selangor Darul Ehsan, Malaysia

Marshall Cavendish is a trademark of Times Publishing Limited
All websites were available and accurate when this book was sent to press.

Library of Congress Cataloging-in-Publication Data

Locricchio, Matthew.
  The cooking of Italy / Matthew Locricchio.
    p. cm. — (Superchef —2nd ed.)
  Includes bibliographical references and index.
  Summary: "Introduces the different culinary regions of Italy and presents many kinds of recipes for traditional Italian dishes"—Provided by publisher.
  ISBN 978-1-60870-554-2 (print) — ISBN 978-1-60870-742-3 (ebook)
1. Cooking, Italian—Juvenile literature. 2. Food habits—Italy—Juvenile literature. I. Title.
  TX723.L585 2012
  641.5945—dc22
          2010051849

Editor: Peter Mavrikis
Publisher: Michelle Bisson
Art Director: Anahid Hamparian
Series design by Kay Petronio
Art direction for food photography by Matthew Locricchio
Food styling by Marie Hirschfeld and Matthew Locricchio

Photo Credits: Russell Kord/Alamy: 14; Art Kowalsky/Alamy: 17; Claudio H. Artman/Alamy: 20; Matthew Locricchio: 61, 69; felinda/Fotolia.com: 90; photka/Fotolia.com: 90, 92, 93; volff/Fotolia.com: 91; Multiart/Fotolia.com: 91; nito/Fotolia.com: 92; Le Do/Fotolia.com: 93; Dmitriy Kosterev/Fotolia.com: 93; rimglow/Fotolia.com: 93; Peter Jameson: 96.

Printed in Malaysia (T)
135642

SUPER CHEF

The Cooking of
ITALY

second edition

Matthew Locricchio

with photos by Jack McConnell

Marshall Cavendish
Benchmark
New York

Contents

Dear Reader,

I can't think of a better way to learn about a culture first-hand than to cook and savor its cuisine. Understanding the breadth of Italian pasta varieties, or Greek phyllo specialties and greens dishes, of Chinese dumplings, Indian curries, Thai spice blends, and more helps us understand something about the geography, history, and soul of a country.

My first memories of food come from my own family, of Sunday meals that lasted half the day and holidays that required a week of cooking. There was a rhythm to the dishes we ate depending on the time of year, with specific sweets for Christmas, breads for New Year's, and the vegan fare my grandmother would prepare as we fasted for Easter. For me, food became synonymous with both communicating and sharing. The dinner table was a time of talking about the issues of the day. The holidays and impromptu visits by family and friends became reason to put a little something on the table for others to enjoy. Those are important lessons to carry through life and they are learned young. As a kid I always helped in the kitchen, regardless of whether I wanted to or not! Thanks to that I learned to cook fairly young, and by the time I was a teenager, I was inviting my friends over to try my own creations.

Young people today are much more food savvy than I was way back in the 1960s and 1970s. Teenagers have a much broader experience with ethnic foods than I ever did. There was no such thing as organic food when I was growing up. We also did not have access to the constant stream of information available today. Ironically, with the overabundance of information out there on food, there is very little real knowledge about how to cook simple, healthy, good food.

The Superchef series of cookbooks aims to do just that and in the process show young people that the world is, indeed, one delicious kitchen where many different cooking traditions flourish.

Cooking is an art, but it's also more than that. People can live without music, paintings, sculpture, and literature, but we can't live without food! So, enjoy the process, but better yet, enjoy sharing it with others.

Diane Kochilas

Consulting chef
Pylos Restaurant, NYC

Diane Kochilas is a chef, author, and teacher. She has published over a dozen cookbooks including, *The Food and Wine of Greece*, *The Greek Vegetarian*, *Meze*, *The Glorious Foods of Greece*, *Mediterranean Grilling* and more. Diane has also made numerous television and radio appearances, and runs a cooking school focusing on traditional Greek recipes, as well as the culture of Greece. To learn more about Diane, go to www.dianekochilas.com.

From the Author

Welcome to the second edition of Superchef. When we first created this series of cookbooks our goal was to introduce new cooks to traditional yet tantalizing recipes from around the world, adapted to work in your kitchen. That goal has not changed.

Young chefs like yourself who discovered Superchef have been learning to cook international recipes with family and friends ever since. The world of satisfying recipes, along with the basic principles of kitchen safety, food handling, and common-sense nutrition is what made Superchef so popular when it was first introduced. Those same goals hold true with the new edition.

Learning to master authentic international recipes and sharing them with family and friends is the motivation behind these cookbooks. This edition offers the invitation to new cooks as well as old to step into the kitchen and start cooking. Within this complete series you will find classic recipes from eight different countries. The recipes are not necessarily all low-fat or low-calorie, but they are all healthful. Even if you are a vegetarian, you will find recipes without meat or with suggestions to make the dish meatless.

Superchef can change the way you feel about cooking. You can learn to make authentic and delicious dishes from recipes that have been tested by young cooks in kitchens like yours. The recipes range from very basic to challenging. The instructions take you through the preparation of each dish step by step. Once you learn the basic techniques of the recipes, you will understand the principles of cooking fresh food successfully.

There is no better way to get to know people than to share a meal with them. Today, more than ever, it is essential to understand the many cultures that inhabit our planet. One way to really learn about a country is to know how its food tastes. Cooking is the one thing we all have in common. You can prepare a recipe in your kitchen and know that somewhere, perhaps many thousands of miles away, that same dish is probably being prepared in the country where it originated.

Every day in the United States we are reminded of our multicultural richness just by the foods available to us. The delicious result of that abundance is that American cooking has developed into one of the most diverse and appealing cuisines on the planet.

Learning to cook is one of the most important things anybody can do. Cooking skills stay with you your entire life and it sure is fun. Learning to cook takes practice, patience, and common sense, but it's not nuclear science. Cooking certainly has its rewards. Just the simple act of preparing food can lift your spirits. Nothing brings family and friends together better than cooking and then sharing the meal you've made. It can be fun, and you get to eat your mistakes. It can even lead to a high-paying career. Most importantly, you can be proud to say, "Oh, glad you liked it. I did it myself."

Happy cooking!

Matthew Locricchio

Matthew Locricchio

A Word about Safety

Safety and common sense are the two most important ingredients in any recipe. Before you begin to make the recipes in this book, take a few minutes to master some simple kitchen safety rules.

Ask an adult to be your assistant chef. To ensure your safety, some steps in a recipe are best done with the help of an adult, like handling pots of boiling water or hot cooking oils. Good cooking is about teamwork. With an adult assistant to help, you've got the makings of a perfect team.

Read the entire recipe before you start to prepare it, and have a clear understanding of how the recipe works. If something is not clear, ask your teammate to explain it.

Dress the part of a chef. Wear an apron. Tie back long hair so that it's out of your food and away from open flames. Why not do what a chef does and wear a clean hat to cover your hair!

Always start with clean hands and a clean kitchen before you begin any recipe. Always wash your hands again after handling raw meat, poultry, or fish. Leave the kitchen clean when you're done.

Pot holders and hot pads are your friends. The hands they save may be your own. Use them only if they are dry. Using wet holders on a hot pot can cause a serious burn!

Keep the handles of the pots and pans turned toward the middle of the stove. That way you won't accidentally hit them and knock over pots of hot food. Always use pot holders to open or move a pan on the stove or in the oven.

🔘 **Remember to turn off the stove and oven when you are finished cooking.** Sounds like a simple idea, but it's easy to forget.

Be Sharp about Knives

🔘 A simple rule about knife safety is that your hands work as a team. One hand grips the handle and operates the knife while the other guides the food you are cutting. The hand holding the food should never come close to the blade of the knife. Keep the fingertips that hold the food slightly curved and out of the path of the blade, and use your thumb to keep the food steady. Go slowly. There is no reason to rush.

🔘 Always hold the knife handle with dry hands. If your hands are wet, the knife might slip.

🔘 Work on a cutting board, never a tabletop or countertop.

🔘 Never place sharp knives in a sink full of soapy water, where they could be hidden from view. Someone reaching into the water might get hurt.

Italian food is all about good flavor. Flavor does not come just from spices, and it is not something that instantly happens when food is cooked. Instead, Italian flavor begins with a strong foundation and builds on it. The good ingredients in Italian dishes are the foundation of unforgettable flavor and the basis of Italian cooking.

It is important to look for the freshest ingredients when you shop for the recipes in this book. If you are not sure something is fresh, just ask. Don't be afraid to inquire when the fish was delivered, or when the vegetables arrived at the market. With a little practice, you will become an expert in recognizing and choosing fresh food, and that is a valuable tool for any cook.

Most importantly, Italian cooking is fun, and it is best when it is shared with family and friends. How can you be sure the recipe you just made came out right? You will know that it is right if it makes you want to smile as you eat it. That's Italian!

Here are a few simple cooking techniques to keep in mind as you follow the recipes in this book:

Chop

To chop means to use a sharp knife to cut food into pieces. Chopping vegetables for recipes can seem like a lot of work. A food processor, if there is one in your kitchen, can make food preparation tasks easier. Ask an adult assistant to help you use the food processor, and be very careful of the sharp blades.

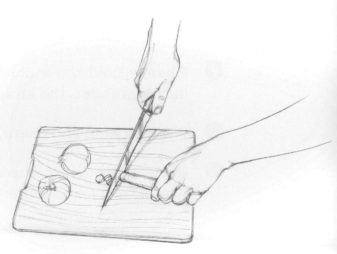

Sauté

To sauté means to lightly fry ingredients in a small amount of fat, butter, or oil, while stirring with a spoon or spatula.

Simmer

Simmering is cooking just below the boiling point. Gentle bubbles will roll lazily to the top of the liquid that is simmering. Simmering brings out maximum flavor and is used frequently in Italian cooking.

Skim

You skim to remove fats or cooking residues as ingredients go from raw to cooked. When you are making soups or sauces, skimming is an important step in reducing fat and enriching flavor.

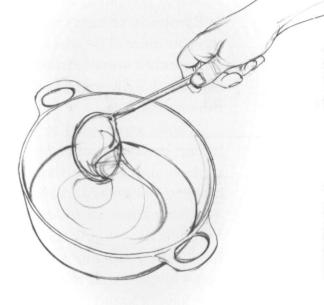

Soffritto

Once the basic ingredients like onions and garlic are sautéed in olive oil or butter, separately or a combination of both, you have a *soffritto*. Making the soffritto is very important in building flavor and should be done carefully, so be sure to give it your full attention. It is essential not to burn the soffritto, because your recipe will pick up the taste of the burned ingredients. If it does burn, you will have to discard the ingredients and start again.

The Regions of Italy and How They Taste

Look at the map of Italy and its shape is instantly recognizable—a boot that has stepped into the Mediterranean and Adriatic seas. Just to make sure it is not going anywhere, that boot is securely fastened to the rest of Europe in the north with the majestic Alps, the tallest mountains on the continent. The Apennine Mountains extend from north to south, creating Italy's spine. Finally, off the tip—or toe—of the Italian boot lie the islands of Sicily and Sardinia, surrounded by the emerald green Mediterranean Sea.

It may seem easy to define Italian cooking in general terms. It's all Italian cooking, right? Not quite. In fact, Italy has some twenty distinct regions, and each of these differs in many ways: land features, climate, history, customs, and ways of cooking. Even the form of Italian spoken and the names for foods and cooking techniques may vary from region to region. So what is the one thing you can say about all Italian cooking? Real Italian cooking is *la cucina di casa*—the cooking of home. It is in the home kitchen that real Italian food is created, based on the unique foods and flavors found in local markets and fields.

For simplicity, we will divide the cooking of Italy into three main areas: north, central, and south, along with the islands of Italy. It will be helpful to remember these divisions as we explore the regions of Italy and how they taste.

The North

The Alps, with their beautiful foothills and rich, fertile river valleys crown Italy's northern border. The Po River, the longest river in Italy, begins its journey here, near the French border. It flows across the north, through the regions of Piedmont, Lombardy, and Emilia-Romagna.

The Po irrigates the lowland plains and provides power for the industrial cities of the north, before ending its 405-mile (652-kilometer)

journey at the Adriatic Sea. Its fertile valley provides Italy with one of its main rice- and grain-growing regions.

The cuisine of the north can be described as lavish, hearty, and sophisticated. The climate consists of cold winters with lots of snow, and the people of the north have created rich, hearty foods to keep the cold out. Minestrone, for example, is a combination of fresh vegetables, pasta, rich broth, and cannellini beans, all slow-cooked with bacon for added flavor. Some call minestrone the most famous of all Italian soups.

Lombardy is home to Lake Garda. Italy's largest and most popular lake is located at the foot of the Alps.

Here in the north polenta is even more popular than pasta. Polenta is a form of cornmeal mush, but to call it mush just doesn't seem fair. It is simply one of the great foods on the planet. Polenta in one form or another has been eaten for over three thousand years in Italy—and for good reason. Served hot with lots of melted butter and grated cheese, it is quite unforgettable. The cooks of the north sometimes slice polenta and brown it in butter, to accompany a main course. It can also be cooked, cooled, cut into slices, and layered with cheese and sausage to make a polenta pie.

Below the splendid mountains of the north is the city of Milan. It is one of the important commercial, financial, and cultural centers of Europe, and is home to the famous opera house La Scala. Milan is known for its restaurants where, alongside traditional food favorites, exciting new dishes flourish. Panettone, a Christmas cake, is a Milanese specialty.

The Italian blend of food and history is also evident in the region of the Veneto and its capital, the city of Venice, which lies on the northwestern shore of the Adriatic Sea. Venice glitters with wondrous palaces like bygone jewels, enchanting all who visit. The canals of Venice surrounding this hypnotic city and breathtaking magical architecture bring millions of tourists to its shores each year. In the center of it all is Saint Mark's Square with its towering structures and the large numbers of pigeons who make it their home. One of the most widely known specialties of Venice is rice and peas with smoked ham. It can only be described as Italian comfort food.

Bridging trade between the Eastern and Western worlds, Venice was once Europe's leading sea power. The renowned chefs of Venice are experts at delicately frying seafood to culinary perfection.

Southwest of Venice is the culinary center of the north, Bologna, where Italy's past and present combine in a bustling modern city in the heart of the Emilia-Romagna region. Some of the most famous dishes in all Italian cooking come from this region. Among them are *ragù alla Bolognese*, a rich, slow-cooked sauce often served over handmade pasta called *tagliatelle*. A key ingredient in this dish is Parmigiano-Reggiano, a cheese from the cities of Parma and Reggio Emilia. To ensure its quality, this golden cheese has been produced under the same strict laws for hundreds of years.

For a taste of the north try: Rice and Peas with Smoked Ham; Pasta Sauce from Bologna; Polenta Pie with Sausage and Cheese; Chicken, Hunters' Style; Asparagus with Parmesan and Butter; and Chocolate and Walnut Cake.

Central Italy

"True to its roots" seems to best describe the cooking of the central region of Italy. Here the Apennine Mountains divide east from west, and each section has its own distinct cooking style.

Tuscany, in the western part of central Italy, is a beautiful and peaceful region. The mountains are covered with chestnut and beech trees. Fresh vegetables and herbs flourish around Florence and Tuscany's other magnificent cities. Tuscan cooks have been creating pastas, vegetable dishes, and remarkable pastries for a very long time.

Olive trees also flourish in the Tuscan hills. The olives that are hand-picked and pressed between massive stone wheels create olive oil that earns the name "cold-pressed, extra-virgin olive oil." This is regarded by food experts as some of the finest olive oil in the world.

The region of Umbria lies just south of Tuscany, and is located on the western slopes of the Apennine Mountains. Umbria's soft, hilly landscape has remained mostly unchanged for centuries, and its people have always had great respect for nature and the land. The traditional dishes of Umbria are prepared simply, using local ingredients, reflecting the region's uncomplicated lifestyle.

Within Umbria is the town of Perugia. Chocolate made in Perugia is regarded as the best in Italy. Chocolate lovers from around the world visit this region to taste Perugia's treasures.

The Marches region, in the eastern half of central Italy, is on the shores of the Adriatic Sea. Once a colony of Rome, the Marches region is known for its beautiful countryside, breathtaking waterfalls, and the dozen or so rivers that run parallel to the sea. Fishermen travel to the Marches port of San Benedetto to fish these waters. San Benedetto, one of Italy's finest ports, supplies over 10 percent of Italy's fresh fish.

Rome and the surrounding Latium region are in the southernmost section of central Italy. Many of the foods of north and south come together here. There are more restaurants in Rome than in any other city in Italy. Eating outside the home is probably a carryover from Rome's past.

Patches of cypress, evergreens, and golden grains crown the magical countryside of Tuscany.

In ancient Rome there was a law—aimed at preventing fires—that forbade anyone who lived in an apartment from having a cooking fire. That law became a tradition that has sent Roman diners to restaurants for centuries. The towns around Rome have their own style of cooking. One dish in particular remains a popular appetizer all over Italy and in restaurants around the world. Toasted bread with tomatoes, known by the Italians as *bruschetta* is instantly recognizable. Bruschetta was created to celebrate the holiday months of December and January with specially baked bread dipped in the new harvest of olive oil, rubbed with garlic, and topped with tomatoes and basil.

For a taste of central Italy try: Pasta with Spring Vegetables; Roman Style Green Beans with Tomatoes; and Toasted Bread with Tomatoes.

The South and the Islands

As you move south into the regions of Abruzzi, Campania, Basilicata, Calabria, and the islands of Sicily and Sardinia, the cooking changes. Vegetable crops change, too. Eggplant, fennel, artichokes, garlic, onions, and tomatoes start to appear more often. Tomatoes thrive in the south's sunny, hot climate, and local cooks make good use of them along with hot peppers. Dried pasta replaces polenta and rice dishes. Olive oil replaces butter as the main cooking fat. Combinations of all these ingredients create some of the most delicate and delicious cooking of Italy.

The Campania region of southern Italy is home to Mount Vesuvius as well as the bustling city of Naples. When the rest of the world thinks of Italian cooking, Naples often comes to mind first. The single biggest reason is one very famous dish—pizza! Naples made pizza a star. The first Neapolitan restaurant opened in New York in 1905, and pizza was an instant hit. Today there is a pizzeria in almost every major city around the globe.

Naples is a noisy, bustling city always on the go. That may be one reason why the Neapolitan chefs created a pizza you can eat on the go right out of your hand. *Calzone,* which means "trouser leg" in Italian, is a baked pizza crust filled with classic ingredients like pepperoni, ricotta, and Parmesan cheese. This dish has become so popular it is served just about everywhere pizza is sold. The other most recognizable Italian food is probably spaghetti and meatballs. It has been canned, frozen, and even freeze-dried, but there is still nothing more delicious than home-made spaghetti and meatballs.

The noisy and lively atmosphere of Naples carries eastward as you travel to the Apulia region, which runs along the coast of the Adriatic Sea. This region is the breadbasket of Italy. It is here that semolina and durum wheat are grown for making pasta. Olives are also grown and harvested for curing and for oil. The olives from this section of the south go into about 40 percent of the olive oil that makes it onto Italian tables and 10 percent of the world's tables. Other delicious treasures that thrive in the region include table grapes, almonds, figs, and citrus fruits. Apulia's coastline is 426 miles (685 km) long, the longest of any region in Italy. It abounds in seafood, which is a large part of the local cuisine.

Bordering Apulia is a secluded and primitive region called Basilicata. This region makes up the arch of the sole on the Italian boot. The local sausages, called *lucanica*, are famous for their spices and flavor. Italians have treasured this regional delicacy since the days of the ancient Romans.

This brings us to the instep and tip of the Italian boot, Calabria. The terrain in this region is dramatic and beautiful. Dense forests of beech, laurel, and pine trees blanket the plateau 1,500 feet (460 meters) above sea level. Winters are cold and the higher elevations can remain buried under snow for at least half the year. Summer temperatures can be very hot. Travel south to the toe, where the land is the narrowest, and you can see both the Tyrrhenian and Ionian seas. On the western coast you can see two active volcanoes.

The people of Calabria will tell you that they have created their own cuisine, untouched by the influences of outsiders. Local cooks claim that eggplant parmigiana, one of the great dishes in Italian cooking, originated in Calabria. The rest of Italy may dispute that claim, but one thing is certain: the cooking of Calabria works magic with eggplants, tomatoes, and cheese.

Italy's true culinary beginnings can be found on the two large islands of Sicily and Sardinia. In ancient times the clever Sicilians and Sardinians borrowed just enough valuable cooking secrets from the Greeks and Phoenicians to create a distinct style of cooking that they eventually taught to the Romans. In ancient Rome it was fashionable for wealthy households to have a Sicilian cook. And as the Roman Empire expanded, the cooking of Sicily and Sardinia spread throughout Italy eventually reaching many other parts of the world.

Sicily is the largest island in the Mediterranean and a place of spectacular beauty. It remains a favorite destination for tourists, because of its well-preserved Greek ruins and its friendly people. Sicily grows an amazing assortment of citrus fruits, olives, grapes, figs, and spices. The tomatoes grown on the island are legendary. The seafood is prized throughout Italy, and Sicilian pastries hold a special place in world cuisine. Festivals, holidays, and the feast days of saints are celebrated with particular delicacies. Cannoli, a cream-filled crispy pastry often served at Christmas, is one of Italy's favorite desserts.

Sardinia was settled before its neighbor Sicily and was invaded less often than other parts of Italy. That may be why Sardinian cooking is like no other in all of Italy. It is a cuisine all its own.

This Sicilian merchant makes final preparations before his regular shoppers arrive to find ingredients perfect for their recipes.

Wheat is Sardinia's chief crop, along with artichokes, onions, tomatoes, grapes, and citrus fruits. Rock lobsters and a wonderful assortment of fish come from the port of Alghero, along the western coast. The Sardinian cook makes a flat, thin, round bread that is baked in sheets, dipped in olive oil, and sprinkled with sea salt. Simple tomato salads made with the island's rich, dark red tomatoes and red onions are the perfect accompaniment to summer meals. Pastas, cheese, and local sausages are used to create dishes you will find nowhere else in Italy. Sardinian pastries are considered works of art. Cakes created to celebrate the feast days of saints are elaborately decorated with intricate lace made from spun sugar.

For a taste of the south and the islands of Italy try: Tomato Salad; Spaghetti and Meatballs; Sicilian Style Swordfish Pasta; Pizza from Naples; Pizza Turnover; and Country-Style Pork.

The cooking of Italy has been written about and savored throughout the world for centuries. Now that you have been introduced to the tastes of the Italian regions, don't you think it's time to start cooking so you can enjoy it, too?

Tortellini soup.

Rich Meat Broth *Il Brodo*

When you look at this recipe and see that it takes three hours to cook, don't turn the page. This rich broth, or stock, is used for making soups and sauces. You will find that many recipes use broth for flavoring instead of plain water. The broth will keep in the refrigerator for three days, or you can freeze it for up to six months. For some more ways to use broth, look at the chef's tip at the end of the recipe.

Makes ½ gallon

Ingredients

2 to 3 pounds beef bones with meat

2 to 3 pounds chicken wings, necks, or thighs (or a combination of all three)

2 stalks celery, broken into large chunks

2 carrots, broken into large chunks

1 onion with skin, cut into quarters

1 large tomato, cut into quarters, or ½ cup canned tomatoes

2 whole cloves garlic with skin

½ cup fresh Italian parsley

10 cups cold water

On your mark, get set, cook!

- Place all the ingredients except the water in a large pot.

- Add the water and bring to a boil. This will take 20 to 30 minutes. As the liquid comes to a boil, use a large spoon to skim off any foam or impurities that rise to the top.

- Cover the pot, leaving the lid slightly open. Reduce the heat to simmer and let cook for 2 to 3 hours.

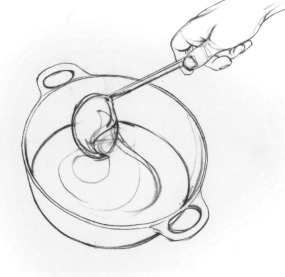

- Turn off the heat. Ask your adult assistant to strain the broth through a colander into a heatproof bowl or pan.

- When the cooked ingredients have cooled enough to handle, discard.

- Let the broth cool and then refrigerate or freeze. Any fat in the broth will collect at the top and should be removed and discarded.

Chef's Tip for making Tortellini Soup

For a simple and flavorful soup, try this: Place 6 cups rich meat broth in a saucepan, add ¼ cup rice, and bring to a boil. Reduce the heat and simmer for 20 minutes, or until the rice is tender. Serve hot with freshly grated Parmesan cheese. Serves 4. Or: Place 4 cups rich meat broth in a saucepan. Add 1 ½ cups frozen tortellini (a pasta filled with meat or cheese, available in Italian food stores or well-stocked supermarkets). Bring to a boil, then reduce the heat and simmer for 12 to 15 minutes, or until the tortellini are just tender. Serve hot with freshly grated Parmesan cheese. Serves 2 to 4.

Vegetable Soup
Il Minestrone

Minestrone means "big hearty soup." You will find different versions of this soup in every region of Italy. This classic recipe comes from Piedmont, in the north of Italy, and is considered by many Italians to be their country's most famous soup. For the broth, try making your own meat broth using the recipe on page 25. You can also use canned low-sodium beef or chicken broth. To make this recipe vegetarian, use vegetable broth and omit the bacon.

Serves 8

Ingredients

2 tablespoons butter

2 tablespoons extra-virgin olive oil

2 slices thick-cut bacon (optional)

1 medium-size onion

2 medium-size potatoes

4 small carrots

3 stalks celery

2 medium-size zucchini

¼ medium-size head savoy or regular cabbage

2 cloves garlic

1 ½ cups canned cannellini beans, drained

1 cup canned chopped Italian tomatoes with the tomato juice

½ tablespoon salt

½ teaspoon freshly ground pepper

6 cups chicken or vegetable broth, either homemade or canned low-sodium

½ cup small dried pasta (small seashell, mini-elbow, or ditalini pasta)

freshly grated Parmigiano-Reggiano cheese for serving

On your mark, get set . . .

- Measure the butter and olive oil and set aside.
- Slice the bacon into small pieces.
- Peel the onion and chop into small pieces.
- Wash and cut the potatoes, unpeeled, in half lengthwise. Lay the flat side down and cut each half into slices, then cut the slices into small chunks.

- Wash the carrots, celery, and zucchini, and chop into bite-size pieces.

- Remove any limp outside leaves from the cabbage. Remove the white core at the base. Cut the cabbage into quarters. Chop the cabbage into small pieces and measure 2 cups.

- Peel and chop the garlic.

Cook!

- In a pot large enough to hold all the ingredients (6- to 8-quart), heat the butter and olive oil over medium-low heat.

- When the butter is melted, add the bacon, onion, and garlic. Cook for 5 to 7 minutes, or until the onion and garlic turn a soft golden color and the bacon just starts to brown.

- Add the potatoes, carrots, celery, zucchini, cabbage, cannellini beans, tomatoes, salt, and pepper. Stir well. Cook for 10 to 12 minutes, stirring occasionally.

- Add the broth. Raise the heat to medium-high and bring to a boil. Skim off any foam that rises to the top. You will need to skim the soup a couple of times as it is cooking.

- Reduce the heat to low, cover the pot with the lid slightly open, and simmer gently for 30 to 40 minutes.

- Add the pasta, raise the heat to medium, and cook for another 8 to 10 minutes, or until the pasta is tender.

- Serve hot with grated Parmigiano-Reggiano cheese.

Chef's Tip

Wash the vegetables very well, especially the zucchini. There is no need to peel them (except the onion). The skins add lots of flavor, color, and nutrients to the soup.

Tomato Salad
Insalata di Pomodoro

There are few foods in the world that combine as well as fresh tomatoes and fresh basil. They just say "summer" when you taste them together. Try this recipe when tomatoes are in season, or when you can find ripe ones with a rich red color in the market. This classic Italian salad is popular in Sardinia, where the tomatoes are so flavorful.

Serves 4

Ingredients

3 medium-size ripe tomatoes

1 medium-size red onion

⅓ cup extra-virgin olive oil

½ teaspoon salt

¼ teaspoon freshly ground pepper

5 or 6 fresh basil leaves

1 tablespoon cold water

On your mark, get set, toss!

- Wash the tomatoes and set them on a cutting board. Cut out the stem circle at the top of each tomato and discard. Cut the tomatoes into small wedges and place them in a bowl.

- Peel the red onion and cut into thin slices, then mix in with the tomatoes.

- Add the olive oil, salt, and pepper. Mix well.

- Wash the basil leaves and tear into small pieces. Add to the salad, along with the 1 tablespoon water.

- Toss well. Don't refrigerate, or the tomatoes will lose their flavor.

Mixed Salad *Insalata Mista*

The Italians have been making salads for a very long time, and that's why they are so good at it. This recipe uses a homemade dressing that will make you think differently about the ones that come prepared in a bottle. Look for the freshest greens you can find. You can be creative with the salad ingredients or follow this recipe. The carrots, sweet red pepper, and celery should be firm and the tomatoes ripe. Remember, the freshest ingredients make the best salads.

Serves 8

Ingredients

SALAD

1 small head romaine lettuce

1 head Boston lettuce

½ bunch fresh spinach (about 6 ounces)

1 small head radicchio

½ sweet red pepper

2 small carrots

2 stalks celery hearts

2 ripe tomatoes

salt and freshly ground pepper to taste

DRESSING

⅓ cup extra-virgin olive oil

1 tablespoon red wine vinegar

1 teaspoon salt

¼ teaspoon sugar

1 clove garlic, crushed

1 teaspoon fresh lemon juice

¼ teaspoon freshly ground pepper

On your mark . . .

- Fill a clean sink with fresh cold water.
- Separate the leaves of the romaine lettuce, the Boston lettuce, the spinach, and the radicchio, and drop them into the water. Let them soak for a few minutes, gently moving them around with your hands to help dislodge any dirt.
- Remove the leaves and place them in a colander. Drain the water from the sink and clean any dirt or sand from the bottom.
- Refill the sink and repeat the washing at least once.

- Use a salad spinner to dry the greens. If you don't have a spinner, lay paper toweling on a clean countertop and place the greens on it. Gently roll up the leaves in the paper towels to absorb the extra moisture. You may have to do this in two batches. You can refrigerate the greens still rolled in the paper towels or use them immediately.

Get set . . .

- Wash and seed the red pepper, and cut into thin slices.

- Wash and peel the carrots, and cut into thin slices.

- Wash the celery hearts and cut into thin slices.

- Wash the tomatoes and cut into wedges.

- To assemble the salad, tear all the greens into bite-size pieces—do not cut them—and place them in a large serving bowl. Add the rest of the salad ingredients. Mix well to combine. Cover with a clean damp cloth and chill until ready to serve.

- For the dressing, combine all the ingredients in a glass jar with a lid, and shake.

Toss!

- When you are ready to serve the salad, remove the garlic clove from the dressing.

- Give the jar another shake and pour the dressing over the salad.

- Add salt and pepper to taste and toss well.

Chef's Tip

Toss the salad with the dressing just before you serve it. That way you'll be sure everything is fresh and crisp.

Toasted Bread with Tomatoes *Bruschetta*

This colorful, crunchy appetizer dates back to the ancient Romans who prepared it for the holiday months of December and January to show off the harvest of fresh extra-virgin olive oil. Originally, course bread slices were dipped in oil then cooked over hot coals. Today the recipe is best known served on slices of oil-rubbed toasted bread topped with fresh tomatoes, basil, and garlic. Bruschetta is easy to put together, which makes it a fool-proof appetizer to prepare at the last minute. Bread is one of the main ingredients in this recipe, so you will want to shop for just the right loaf. Crusty Italian bread, such as *ciabatta*, or a French bread, such as a baguette, will work best.

Serves 4

Ingredients

2 garlic cloves

2 to 3 whole ripe organic local tomatoes or 10 to 12 cherry or grape tomatoes

5 or 6 fresh basil leaves

4 large slices bread, such as Italian ciabatta, peasant bread, French bread, or baguette

⅓ cup extra-virgin olive oil

sea salt

freshly ground black pepper

On your mark . . .

- Slightly crush the garlic by laying the flat side of a chef's knife on the clove and pressing firmly to break open the skin. Remove the skin and set aside.

- Wash the tomatoes, cut out the stem circle at the top and discard. Chop the tomatoes into bite size chunks. Place in a medium-size bowl and set aside.

- Wash the basil leaves, shake to remove the excess water, and dry the sprigs by rolling them in paper towels. Tear the basil leaves into small pieces and set aside.

Get set . . .

- Lay the bread slices on a baking tray and toast under a broiler for 1 to 2 minutes on each side until golden and crispy. Be careful not to burn them.

- Remove the slices. Rub one side with the garlic clove.

Serve!

- On top of each slice, spoon the chopped tomatoes and basil. Drizzle with olive oil. Sprinkle on the sea salt and freshly ground black pepper to taste.

- Serve warm.

Pasta, Pizza, Polenta, and Rice

Pasta is the food of the future. Pasta is also the food of the past. This simple and amazing staple of the Italian kitchen has been a favorite across Italy and throughout the world for centuries. It will probably remain so for many more centuries to come.

Since pasta is made with just two basic ingredients, flour and water, nobody can agree on when or where it was first created. There is an old theory that the Venetian traveler Marco Polo brought it back to Italy from China in the thirteenth century. Many food historians, however, now believe that pasta was already being made in Italy years before Marco Polo's travels. There is another theory that pasta was made thousands of years ago on the islands of Sicily and Sardinia, where wheat was commonly grown.

No matter what theory you believe, one thing is certain: pasta is loved everywhere because it is a nearly perfect food.

Pasta is packed with carbohydrates and vitamins B1, B2, and niacin. Even better news is that in 4 ounces of cooked dried pasta there are only

325 calories. Fresh pasta has 365 calories in 4 ounces. So it is not true, as some people believe, that pasta makes you fat.

When shopping for pasta, be creative. You don't have to buy just spaghetti. Believe it or not, there are more than three hundred varieties of pasta, in all shapes and sizes, from which to choose. Pasta is sold in two ways: dried and fresh. Fresh, or *pasta fresca*, is made with flour and water, usually mixed with eggs. It needs to be used fairly soon after you buy it. Dried pasta, or *pasta asciutta*, is a mixture of flour and water that is dried before being sold. It can be stored for a long time.

How to Cook Pasta

- Begin with a big pot. It should be deep. Pasta loves plenty of water to move around in as it cooks. That way it will cook evenly and won't stick together.

- Add salt to the cold water, about ½ teaspoon for every quart of water.

- Cover the pot and bring the water to a full rolling boil.

- Remove the cover.

- Add the pasta and return the water to a boil. Cook uncovered.

- Check the package instructions for the exact length of cooking time. Set a timer.

- Every so often stir the pasta. If necessary, lower the temperature so the water does not boil too fast. The water should boil fast enough to keep the pasta moving, but not so fast that it boils over.

- When the pasta is cooked, ask your adult assistant to help you strain it through a colander in the sink.

- Never rinse the pasta.

Your pasta is now ready for the sauce. There are two ways you can serve pasta. One way is in a large bowl, family style. The other way is in individual bowls or on plates. The first step is always the same, no matter how you serve it. Place the drained pasta in a large bowl. Add a cup or so of the sauce and toss well to coat the strands. For family style, add more sauce on top and serve. For individual servings, place a single portion of sauced pasta on each plate, top with extra sauce, and serve. You can pass more sauce at the table but remember that Italians never put on a lot of sauce, because they want to taste the pasta, too.

Pasta with Spring Vegetables

Pasta alla Primavera con Asparagi e Cipolle

The Italians have a way with vegetables. Not only do they grow some of the most perfect vegetables in the world, they also are experts at preparing them. Here is a recipe from Florence that combines a few simple vegetables into an exciting and flavorful pasta sauce. This style of preparing vegetables dates back to a Renaissance cooking technique. After you taste this dish, you will understand why it is still being prepared today.

Serves 6

Ingredients

1 small red onion

1 clove garlic

1 stalk celery

1 medium-size carrot

½ pound Swiss chard

1 pound fresh asparagus

1 pound fresh tomatoes

1 medium-size zucchini

3 tablespoons extra-virgin olive oil

2 teaspoons salt

freshly ground pepper to taste

½ cup vegetable or chicken broth, either homemade or canned low-sodium

5 or 6 fresh basil leaves, torn into small pieces

½ teaspoon dried oregano

salt for cooking pasta

1 pound dried spaghetti or linguine

On your mark, get set . . .

- Peel the red onion and chop into small pieces.

- Peel and chop the garlic.

- Wash and scrub the outside skins of the celery and carrot, and chop into small pieces.

- Wash the Swiss chard stalks and cut into ½-inch pieces, and cut or tear the leaves into thin slices.

- Rinse the asparagus with cold water and cut into 1-inch pieces.

- Wash the tomatoes and cut into small chunks.

- Wash the zucchini and cut into chunks.

Cook!

- Heat the olive oil in a 12-inch skillet over low heat. Add the red onion, garlic, celery, and carrot. Sauté for 10 minutes.

- Add the Swiss chard, asparagus, tomatoes, zucchini, 2 teaspoons of salt, and pepper, and carefully mix together all the ingredients.

- Add the vegetable or chicken broth, torn basil leaves, and oregano. Cook for 30 minutes on low heat or a gentle simmer.

- While the sauce is cooking, bring a large pot of cold salted water to a boil.

- Cook the spaghetti according to the package directions.

- When the spaghetti is *al dente*, have your adult assistant help you strain it through a colander. Pour the spaghetti into a large serving bowl.

- Spoon one ladle of the hot sauce over the spaghetti and mix well, coating all the strands with the sauce.

- Pour the rest of the sauce over the top, toss together, and serve immediately.

Chef's Tip

Al dente literally means "to the tooth." It means the pasta is just a little hard and chewy, not very soft. That is the way Italians usually like to eat their pasta.

Spaghetti and Meatballs
Spaghetti con Polpetti di Carne

Is there any dish more loved than spaghetti and meatballs? This classic recipe comes from Naples. The sauce has a real old-fashioned, slow-cooked flavor. Once you taste your homemade sauce and meatballs, you will want to make this dish again and again.

Serves 4 to 6

Ingredients

MEATBALLS

½ pound sweet Italian sausage (3 links)

½ pound ground round beef

2 eggs, lightly beaten

½ cup plain bread crumbs

2 tablespoons chopped Italian flat-leaf parsley

1 tablespoon chopped yellow onion

½ cup freshly grated Parmesan cheese

1 clove garlic, peeled and chopped

¼ teaspoon grated nutmeg (optional)

½ tablespoon salt

4 tablespoons extra-virgin olive oil for frying

SAUCE

2 cloves garlic

1 can (5.5 ounces) tomato paste

2 cans (28 ounces) chopped tomatoes

1 medium-size yellow onion

¼ cup extra-virgin olive oil

2 cups chicken broth, either homemade or canned low-sodium

½ tablespoon dried oregano

½ tablespoon salt

freshly ground pepper to taste

1 pound dried spaghetti

salt for cooking pasta

On your mark . . .

- For the meatballs: Remove the casing from the sausage links. To do this, place 1 sausage on a cutting board and make a slit in the casing the length of the sausage with the tip of a sharp knife. Peel away the casing and discard.

- Using the flat side of the knife, spread the sausage meat onto the surface of the cutting board, then chop it to break up the meat into small pieces.

- Repeat with the other links. Wash the cutting board.

- In a large bowl mix together all the ingredients for the meatballs, except the olive oil. If using your hands to do the mixing, make sure they are very clean. Refrigerate the meatball mixture.

- For the sauce: Peel and chop the garlic. Open the cans of tomato paste and tomatoes. Peel the onion and chop into small pieces.

Get set . . .

- Heat ¼ cup extra-virgin olive oil in a 10-inch skillet over low heat. Add the garlic and cook slowly for 1 minute. If the garlic begins to brown, lower the heat.

- Add the onion and cook slowly for 5 to 6 minutes, or until it changes from white to almost clear.

Cook!

- Place a large pot (8-quart) on the stove and add the cooked garlic and onion.

- Turn the heat to medium. Cook for 1 minute.

- Raise the heat to medium-high and add the tomato paste. Cook for 1 to 2 minutes, using a long-handled spoon to gently stir the mixture. Be careful not to splash yourself.

- Add the chicken broth and cook for another 5 minutes, stirring occasionally.

- Add the chopped tomatoes and bring to a boil. This will take about 10 minutes.

- When the sauce starts to boil, reduce the heat to medium and cook for 30 minutes, stirring occasionally. Use a large metal spoon to skim off the light-colored foam that rises to the top of the pot.

- Add the oregano, salt, and pepper.

- While the sauce is cooking, you can shape and brown the meatballs. Wash your hands. Scoop up a tablespoon of the meat mixture and roll it between the palms of your hands to shape it into a ball about 1 ½ inches wide. For 6 servings make the meatballs 1 inch wide. If the mixture is too wet, add more bread crumbs. Place the meatballs on a tray as you form them.

- Heat a 10-inch skillet over medium-low heat and add 2 tablespoons of the olive oil. Brown the meatballs in the skillet, 4 at a time, using tongs to turn them as they brown. Add the remaining 2 tablespoons olive oil to the skillet as needed, to keep the meatballs from sticking. Place the meatballs on a plate.

- After the sauce has cooked for 30 minutes, add the meatballs to the pot and cook on medium heat for another 45 minutes.

- Cook the spaghetti in a large pot of salted water according to the package directions.

- With the help of your adult assistant, strain the spaghetti through a colander and place in a large serving bowl.

- Add about 1 cup of the sauce and toss to coat the strands.

- Serve the spaghetti on individual plates, spooning additional sauce on each and topping with 2 or 3 meatballs.

Tomato Sauce
Sugo di Pomodoro

Here is a simple recipe for tomato sauce that you can use not only with your favorite pasta, but as a topping for pizza, too. It is the perfect quick sauce to make in the summer, when tomatoes are at their peak of flavor. You can make it any time of the year, though, using canned Italian tomatoes, which work just as well as the fresh. Try adding cooked chicken, fresh vegetables, or seafood to the sauce. This recipe makes about 3 cups of sauce, enough for 1 pound of cooked pasta.

Serves 4

Ingredients

2 pounds ripe tomatoes or 1 can (28 ounces) chopped Italian tomatoes

1 medium-size red or yellow onion

2 cloves garlic

¼ cup fresh basil leaves (optional)

¼ cup extra-virgin olive oil

2 teaspoons dried oregano

1 teaspoon sugar

2 teaspoons salt

freshly ground pepper to taste

On your mark, get set . . .

- Wash the tomatoes and set them on a cutting board. Cut out the stem circle at the top of each tomato and discard. Chop the tomatoes and place in a bowl.

- Peel and chop the onion and garlic.

- If using fresh basil, wash the leaves to remove any dirt and tear into small pieces.

Cook!

- Place a 4-quart saucepan over low heat and add the olive oil, onion, and garlic.

- Sauté for 4 to 5 minutes, or until the onion and garlic turn golden. This is the soffritto. Be careful not to burn it. If you do, you must discard the ingredients and start over, or your finished sauce will have a bitter taste.

- Add the tomatoes, basil, oregano, sugar, salt, and pepper.

- Continue to cook for 20 to 30 minutes, stirring occasionally. The sauce is ready when the color has softened and the flavor is sweet and creamy.

Chef's Tip

Try adding 1 pound of fresh shrimp to the sauce. Wash, peel, and remove the vein from the shrimp. When the sauce is ready, add the shrimp to the saucepan, cooking just until it turns pink (about 2 minutes). Toss with cooked pasta. This sauce is also perfect over polenta.

Pasta Sauce from Bologna
Ragū alla Bolognese

Here is a truly classic Italian recipe. This sauce from the northern city of Bologna may be the most famous of all Italian pasta sauces. It is so famous that nearly every Bolognese will have his or her own version of just how it should be made. There is even the "official" recipe that hangs in Bologna's city hall. Don't be put off by the long cooking time. The slow cooking of this *ragū* produces its great flavor. This sauce is even better the day after you make it, but who can wait a day to eat it?

Serves 6

Ingredients

1 stalk celery

1 carrot

1 medium-size onion

1 can (28 ounces) crushed tomatoes

2 slices bacon (2 to 3 ounces)

3 links sweet Italian sausage (½ pound)

3 tablespoons butter

2 tablespoons extra-virgin olive oil

½ pound ground beef chuck

1 teaspoon salt

1 cup chicken broth, either homemade or canned low-sodium

2 tablespoons tomato paste

¼ teaspoon ground nutmeg (optional)

½ cup whole milk

freshly ground pepper to taste

salt for cooking pasta

1 pound dried pappardella or penne pasta

freshly grated Parmigiano-Reggiano cheese for serving

On your mark . . .

- Wash and finely chop the celery and carrot. Measure ½ cup each.
- Peel and chop the onion and measure ¾ cup.
- Open the canned tomatoes.

Get set . . .

- Chop the bacon into small chunks, all about the same size.
- Remove the casing from the sausage links. To do this, place

1 sausage on a cutting board and make a slit in the casing the length of the sausage with the tip of a sharp knife. Peel away the casing and discard.

- Using the flat side of the knife, spread the sausage meat onto the surface of the cutting board, then chop it to break up the meat into small pieces.

- Repeat with the other links. Wash the cutting board.

Cook!

- Place a 6-quart pot over low heat and add the butter, olive oil, and onion.

- Cook for 2 to 3 minutes.

- Add the celery and carrot and cook for another 2 to 3 minutes.

- Add the bacon and cook for 1 minute.

- Raise the heat to medium. Add the ground beef, sausage meat, and 1 teaspoon of salt. Cook until the meat has lost its red color, about 3 to 4 minutes.

- Add ½ cup of the chicken broth and cook for 3 to 4 minutes.

- Add the tomatoes, tomato paste, nutmeg, milk, and pepper.

- Add the remaining ½ cup chicken broth.

- When the sauce starts to bubble, reduce the heat to simmer. Cook slowly for at least 1 to 1 ½ hours. Stir occasionally.

- About 30 minutes into the cooking, skim off the oil that rises to the top and discard it.

- About 20 minutes before the sauce is done, boil a large pot of salted water and cook the pasta according to the package directions.

- Strain the pasta with the help of your adult assistant and place in a serving bowl. Toss with a small amount of the sauce to coat the strands.

- Spoon the rest of the sauce over the pasta and serve with grated Parmigiano-Reggiano cheese on the side.

Swordfish Pasta, Sicilian Style
Pasta con Pescespada alla Siciliana

The island of Sicily is rich with exotic flavors and local specialties. Here's a classic fresh fish recipe that is still served in the port city of Palermo. Sicilians are outstanding seafood cooks, because there is such a great variety of fish available from the three seas that surround their beautiful island. Look for the freshest boneless fish steaks you can find when preparing this dish. If swordfish is not available, you can substitute tuna, red snapper, or salmon.

Serves 6

Ingredients

4 fresh boneless swordfish steaks (about 28 to 32 ounces total)

1 small onion (about ¾ cup chopped)

2 cloves garlic

1 stalk celery

½ cup currants or raisins

⅓ cup pine nuts or chopped walnuts

2 teaspoons salt

freshly ground pepper to taste

1 pound fresh tomatoes (about 2 cups chopped)

8 to 10 fresh basil leaves

½ cup pitted green or black olives

1 tablespoon capers

1 fresh orange

salt for cooking pasta

1 pound dried penne pasta or spaghetti

3 tablespoons extra-virgin olive oil

On your mark, get set . . .

- Wash the fish steaks under cold water and pat dry. If there is any skin on the fish steaks, remove it.
- Cut the fish into 2-inch cubes, place in a bowl, and refrigerate until ready to use. Wash the cutting board.
- Peel and chop the onion and measure ¾ cup.

- Crush, peel, and chop the garlic.

- Wash and chop the celery, measure ¾ cup, and set aside.

- Measure the currants, nuts, and salt. Place these ingredients and the pepper close to the onion, garlic, and celery, but don't combine.

- Wash the tomatoes. Cut out the stem circle at the top of each tomato and discard. Chop into small chunks, measure 2 cups, and place in a medium-size bowl.

- Wash and tear the basil leaves into small pieces and add to the tomatoes.

- Chop the olives into small pieces and add to the bowl.

- Rinse the capers in a small hand strainer and add those as well.
- Squeeze the juice from the orange, removing any pits, and add to the bowl.
- Stir together until well combined.

Cook!

- Bring a large pot (6- to 8-quart) of cold salted water to a boil for the pasta. Cook the pasta according to the package directions.
- In the meantime, heat the olive oil in a skillet (10- to 12-inch) over low heat. Add the onion, garlic, celery, currants, nuts, salt, and pepper. Cook for 3 to 4 minutes.
- Raise the heat to medium and add the tomato mixture to the skillet. Cook for 10 minutes.
- Reduce the heat to low and add the fish cubes. Mix well with a spoon to make sure all the ingredients are combined.
- Add about ½ cup of the pasta cooking water to the skillet. Cook for 10 to 15 minutes, or until the fish is tender.
- Get your adult assistant to help you strain the pasta into a colander.
- Pour the pasta into a serving bowl and add the fish and sauce. Toss together gently, and the dish is ready to serve.

Pizza Dough *La Pasta da Pizza*

Here is a recipe for pizza dough that can also make delicious bread. When preparing any recipe with flour and yeast, it is important to have extra flour close by. You will need to sprinkle it on the work surface when you knead the dough. You may also need a tablespoon or so more than the recipe calls for. Lots of things, such as humidity, altitude, and the age of the flour, can affect how much flour you'll need for the dough.

This recipe makes two 10-inch pizzas or one large loaf of bread.

Ingredients

1 ¼ cups warm water (100°F-110°F)

1 package (¼ ounce) active dry yeast

3 level cups unbleached all-purpose flour

½ level tablespoon salt

1 tablespoon extra-virgin olive oil

extra flour for kneading

extra olive oil for the bowl

On your mark . . .

- Measure ¼ cup of the warm water into a small bowl. Make sure the water is not too hot, which will stop the yeast from becoming active, or too cool, which will keep it from starting. Use a kitchen thermometer or run the water over your fingers for a few seconds to make sure it is just warm.

- Sprinkle the package of yeast over the water, give it a stir, and then cover it.

- The water and yeast combination will need 10 minutes to become active. You will know the yeast is active if after 10 minutes soft bubbles appear on the surface of the water. If the bubbles do not appear, you'll need to start over with a new package of yeast and fresh water.

Get set . . .

- Place 3 cups flour in a large bowl and sprinkle the salt over the flour.

- With a spoon make a well in the center of the flour. Pour the active yeast and water into the well. Mix with a fork until a wet paste forms.

- Combine the remaining 1 cup warm water and 1 tablespoon of olive oil. Pour into the bowl and mix all the ingredients together. You should now have soft dough.

- Sprinkle a tablespoon of flour on a clean work surface. Sprinkle extra flour on your hands to keep the dough from sticking to them. Remove the dough from the bowl and place it on the work surface.

- Begin kneading by pressing the dough away from you with the palms of your hands and then folding it in half. Pick it up and give it a turn to the right or left. Work the dough over and over for 5 to 6 minutes, repeating that same action. Be sure to keep turning the dough in the same direction. It will be sticky in the beginning, but don't worry.

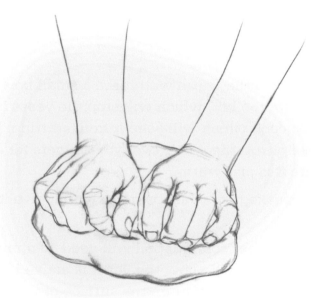

- From time to time, give the dough a few punches to get the air out. Knead until it is smooth and springy. Now it is ready for a rest.

- Drizzle a small amount of olive oil into a clean bowl and place the dough on top of it. Give the ball of dough a few spins and turn it over to lightly coat it with the oil.

- Cover with a sheet of plastic wrap and a couple of heavy, clean kitchen towels.

- Place the dough in a warm, draft-free spot where it can rise undisturbed for 1 ½ hours, or until it doubles in size.

Cook!

- To make the dough into pizza, follow the recipe on page 58.

- To make the dough into bread: Sprinkle a little flour on your hands. Pull the dough out of the bowl and punch it down to remove air. Knead again for 4 to 6 minutes on a lightly floured work surface.

- Shape the dough to fit into a lightly oiled 8 ½ x 4 ½-inch bread pan. Brush the top with a little olive oil.

- Cover with plastic wrap or wax paper and heavy, clean kitchen towels. Let the bread rise again in a warm, draft-free spot for 1 hour.

- Preheat the oven to 375°F.

- Bake for 50 to 60 minutes.

- Remove the bread from the oven and let it cool for a few minutes. Using clean hot pads carefully tip the pan over and remove the bread. The bread will make a hollow sound when you tap it and that means it's done. If it's not done, return it to the bread pan and bake another 5 to 10 minutes.

Pizza from Naples
Pizza Napoletana

Everybody loves pizza! It is simply one of the most popular foods on the planet today. There are as many varieties of pizza and toppings as the imagination will allow. Why not try making pizza at home? It's fun to make and even more fun to eat. This simple version from Naples, made with a few delicious toppings, will have you saying, "Homemade is best!"

Serves 4

Ingredients

1 ½ cups canned chopped Italian tomatoes

½ pound mozzarella cheese

1 tablespoon extra-virgin olive oil

2 teaspoons dried oregano

8 anchovy fillets (optional)

extra olive oil for the pan

1 recipe pizza dough (page 55)

freshly ground pepper to taste

On your mark . . .

- Preheat the oven to 450°F.

- Drain the tomatoes in a hand strainer and shake off any excess liquid.

- Grate the mozzarella into a bowl, using the large holes of a cheese grater.

- Add the olive oil to the cheese and toss.

- Measure the oregano into a small bowl.

- If using the anchovies, drain off any excess oil and separate the fillets on a plate. Tear the fillets into small pieces.

- Lightly oil an 11 x 16-inch baking pan or cookie sheet.

Get set . . .

- If making one large pizza, keep the dough in one piece. If making two smaller pizzas, divide the dough and the topping ingredients in half. Cover one half of the dough as you prepare the other half.

- Place the dough on the baking pan and, using your fingers and the palms of your hands, press and push the dough to stretch it to cover the pan. Try not to tear it. If you do tear the dough, simply give it a pinch at the torn spot to repair it. Don't worry if the shape is not exact. Remember, your pizza is made by hand, so it should not have a perfect shape.

- After you get the dough about ¼ inch thick, use your fingers to make lots of tiny dents all across the surface.
- Top with the tomatoes, spreading them across the dough. Then add the mozzarella.
- If using the anchovies, press them into the dough.
- Sprinkle with the oregano and a little pepper. The pizza is ready to bake.

Cook!

- Bake for 25 to 30 minutes, or until the crust is brown and crispy at the edges.
- Slice and serve hot.

Chef's Tip

You can also add sliced pepperoni, fresh basil, pitted black olives, or grated Parmesan cheese to your pizza toppings.

Pizza Turnover *Calzone*

Sometimes you just want your pizza to go. Here is the original portable pizza that comes from the region of Campania and the famous city of Naples. This recipe uses the pizza dough on page 55, or, if you want to save time, you can choose to buy pizza dough already prepared. But remember—nothing beats homemade! Waiting for calzone to cool when it first comes out of the oven takes some patience. But once you break it open and take that first bite it's all so worth it. *Calzone* means "trouser leg" in Italian and maybe that's why it gets around so much!

Serves 4

Ingredients

1 generous cup (8 ounces) shredded mozzarella

½ cup (4 ounces) ricotta cheese

½ cup (2 ounces) grated Parmesan cheese

1 teaspoon dried oregano

¼ cup canned Italian-style plum tomatoes with liquid

1 clove peeled garlic

1 pizza dough recipe (page 55) or ready-made pizza dough

3 tablespoons extra-virgin olive oil

2 ounces sliced pepperoni (about 1 cup) or sliced Genoa salami

4 to 5 fresh basil leaves (optional)

1 teaspoon salt

freshly ground black pepper or red pepper flakes

parchment paper for baking the calzone

On your mark . . .

- Combine the mozzarella, ricotta, 1 ounce of the Parmesan cheese, and ½ teaspoon of the dried oregano, in a large bowl. Mix well to combine all the ingredients and set to the side.

- Pour the canned tomatoes and garlic into the jar of a blender. Press the lid firmly into place. Blend at high speed for about 15 seconds or until you have a smooth puree.

- Pour into a small bowl and set to the side.

Get set . . .

- Preheat oven to 500°F.

- If using the salami, stack the slices into a couple of short piles. Cut each pile into strips about ½ inch wide. Set the salami to the side.

- Place the parchment paper on the baking tray and lightly oil the sheet. You may have to fold the edges under to make the paper lay flat on the tray. Set the baking tray to the side.

- Lightly flour a cutting board or clean countertop.

- Sprinkle a little of the flour on the pizza dough and lightly coat it with the flour. Cut the dough into 4 equal portions.

- Using your fingers and the palms of your hands, press each portion of the dough into a 6-inch circle.

- Brush the surface of the circles with some of the olive oil, leaving a 1-inch border without oil. Spread ¼ of the cheese mixture on the bottom half of each of the dough circles, making sure to leave the 1-inch border clear of cheese.

- Add ¼ of the pepperoni circles or salami strips to the bottom half of each circle. Tear the basil leaves in half and place them on top

of the cheese. Sprinkle on ¼ teaspoon of the salt and pepper on each circle.

- Brush the 1-inch border of the dough where there is no filling with water.

- Pull the unfilled half of the dough over the filled half.

- Roll the edges of the dough together and press down with your fingers to seal it. Using the tines of a fork, press the edges again to help make an even tighter seal. This extra step will keep the filling from leaking during baking.

- Carefully lift each calzone onto the baking tray.

- Brush the top with the olive oil.

- Brush each calzone with the remaining tomato puree.

- Sprinkle on the remaining oregano and the rest of the Parmesan cheese.

- Using a sharp knife, cut 3 short slits into each calzone. This will allow air to escape during baking.

Cook!

- Place the baking tray on the middle rack of the oven. Bake for 12 to 14 minutes.

- Remove from the tray with a spatula and place the calzone on a cutting board. Cut in half with a sharp knife.

- Serve hot.

Chef's Tip

Ready-made pizza dough may be purchased at a pizzeria or bakery in your neighborhood. You can also find it frozen at your local supermarket.

Instant Polenta
Polenta Veloce

If you really want to experience northern Italian cooking, you must try polenta. Polenta is made from specially ground corn, and it requires a long, slow cooking time. Instant polenta cooks in much less time. Once you discover how many great meals you can create with polenta, you will know why it is such a popular part of Italian cooking. Follow the suggestions at the end of the recipe for even more ideas for cooking with polenta.

Serves 6

Ingredients

6 ½ cups water

½ tablespoon salt

2 tablespoons extra-virgin olive oil

2 cups Italian instant polenta

On your mark, get set, cook!

- Bring the water, salt, and olive oil to a full boil in a nonstick 6-quart saucepan.

- Rinse a 10-inch square glass baking saucepan with cold water, but don't dry it. Keep it ready next to the stove.

- When the liquid boils, remove the pan from the stove. Pour the polenta into the boiling liquid in a thin, steady stream and stir with a wooden spoon or a whisk. Be alert that you don't splash yourself with the polenta as it cooks.

- Return the saucepan to the stove, cover, and cook for 12 to 15 minutes on low heat. Stir the polenta for another minute after the cooking time has finished.

- Pour the polenta into the wet baking pan. Smooth the surface of the hot polenta with a spoon or rubber spatula so that it is all the same thickness.

- Allow the polenta to cool and become firm. The polenta can be cut into ½-inch-thick slices and used in polenta pie with sausage and cheese (page 65).

- Wrap any leftover polenta, refrigerate, and use within 1 week.

Other serving suggestions

- When the polenta has finished cooking, add 3 tablespoons of butter and ½ cup freshly grated Parmigiano-Reggiano cheese. Mix well and serve immediately.

- Fry polenta slices in 1 tablespoon of olive oil and 1 tablespoon of butter combined.

- Brown the slices for about 3 to 4 minutes on each side, turning carefully with a spatula. Serve as a side dish or top with your favorite pasta sauce and grated cheese.

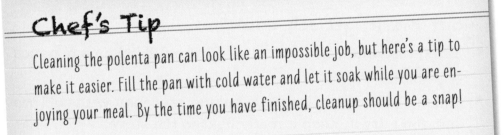

Chef's Tip

Cleaning the polenta pan can look like an impossible job, but here's a tip to make it easier. Fill the pan with cold water and let it soak while you are enjoying your meal. By the time you have finished, cleanup should be a snap!

Polenta Pie with Sausage and Cheese
Polenta al Forno con Salsicce

Winters in the Piedmont region of northern Italy can be cold. A hearty dish like this polenta pie is just the thing to keep the chill out. Polenta is also a great way to use leftover pasta sauces. This recipe is excellent when you have a lot of friends over for dinner. It can easily be doubled to make two pies. You choose the pasta sauce you like best to go into the filling of this layered pie.

Serves 6

Ingredients

PIE SHELL

1 recipe instant polenta (page 63),
  cooked and cooled

FILLING

1 pound sweet Italian sausage (6 links)

1 medium-size yellow onion

4 ounces fontina cheese

4 ounces mozzarella cheese

2 ounces Parmesan cheese

½ cup homemade or bottled pasta sauce

2 teaspoons extra-virgin olive oil

On your mark, get set . . .

- Prepare the instant polenta. Cool until firm and cut into ½-inch-thick slices. Set aside.

- Remove the casings from the Italian sausage. Place 1 link on a cutting board and, with the tip of a sharp knife, make a cut along the length of the sausage. The meat will separate from the casing. Peel away the casing and discard.

- Using the flat side of the knife, spread the sausage meat onto the surface of the cutting board, then chop it to break up the meat into small pieces.

- Repeat with the other links. Wash the cutting board.

- Peel and chop the onion.

- Grate the fontina and mozzarella cheeses, using the large holes of a cheese grater, and combine in a bowl.

- Grate the Parmesan cheese, using the smallest holes, and set aside.

- Measure out the pasta sauce and set aside.

Cook!

- Preheat the oven to 400°F.

- Heat the olive oil in a 10-inch skillet over low heat. Add the onion and cook for 3 to 4 minutes.

- Add the sausage meat and cook for 5 to 6 minutes, or until the meat has lost its red color.

- Remove the sausage and onion from the pan with a slotted spoon to a clean bowl and set aside.

- To assemble the pie, arrange some of the polenta slices so that they completely cover the bottom and sides of a 10-inch square baking pan or cast-iron skillet.

- Sprinkle ¼ cup of the fontina and mozzarella cheese mixture evenly across the bottom layer of polenta. Top with the sausage and onion.

- Spoon on the pasta sauce, then sprinkle on the rest of the fontina and mozzarella.

- Use the remaining polenta slices to form the top layer of the pie. The total amount of polenta you use will vary depending on the size of your pan, so don't worry if you have leftover polenta.

- Sprinkle the grated cheese over the top.

- Bake for 35 to 40 minutes. Cut into slices and serve hot.

Chef's Tip

To make the pie ahead of time, follow the recipe to prepare all the ingredients, and let them chill completely in the refrigerator before you assemble them into the pie. Once the pie is assembled, you can refrigerate it for up to 3 hours. Increase the baking time by 10 to 15 minutes.

Rice and Peas with Smoked Ham *Risi e Bisi*

This dish was created hundreds of years ago for the banquets celebrating the Venetian feast of Saint Mark's. Not surprisingly it remains a Venetian specialty today. Rice and peas with smoked ham will introduce you to the short-grained rice called *arborio,* which usually requires time-consuming steps of standing over the stove and stirring the rice in a simmering broth until tender. This recipe is easier to prepare and just as satisfying than the slow-cooked version. Get ready to fall in love with its exceptional taste.

Serves 4 to 6

Ingredients

6 ounce piece of smoked ham

1 medium yellow onion

1 clove garlic

1 ½ cups frozen baby peas

3 cups chicken stock, either homemade or canned low-sodium

2 tablespoons butter

2 tablespoons extra-virgin olive oil

1 cup Italian arborio rice or any short-grain rice

¾ cup freshly grated Parmesan cheese

On your mark, get set . . .

- Slice the ham into long strips about ½ inch wide. Cut each strip into small cubes and set aside.

- Peel and finely chop the onion, measure ¾ cup and set aside.

- Peel and chop the garlic and set aside.

- Measure 1 ½ cups of peas. Return them to the freezer until ready to use.

Cook!

- In a 3-quart saucepan bring the chicken stock to a boil. Once it boils reduce the heat to simmer.

- In the meantime melt 2 tablespoons of the butter over medium heat with the olive oil in a medium size saucepan with lid.

- Add the chopped onion and garlic and sauté for 1 to 2 minutes. Reduce the heat if the onions and garlic start to brown.

- Remove the peas from the freezer and add them to the pan along with the chopped ham and the rice. Stir well and cook for 2 minutes.

- Raise the heat to medium-high and using a soup ladle add about 2 cups of the simmering chicken stock.

- Bring the rice to a boil and cook uncovered for 5 minutes. Stir occasionally. If the rice begins to boil too fast reduce the heat to medium.

- After 5 minutes add the rest of the stock and return the pan to a boil again.

- Lower the heat to simmer, cover, and cook for 15 minutes. Set a timer so you don't forget.

- Remove the lid and stir in the freshly grated cheese.

- Serve hot.

Hunter's style chicken with pasta.

Chicken, Hunters' Style
Pollo alla Cacciatora

Nearly every region of Italy has a version of this dish. Although the technique of slow-cooking meats in a flavorful sauce is found all over Italy, this recipe is inspired by the cooking of the Veneto region. Serve this recipe on its own or over pasta or pan-fried polenta.

Serves 4

Ingredients

3 ½ pounds chicken (preferably organic), cut into 8 pieces

½ cup all-purpose flour

3 ½ teaspoons salt

freshly ground pepper to taste

1 small yellow onion

1 carrot

1 clove garlic

4 ounces fresh mushrooms

½ cup canned chopped tomatoes

2 ½ tablespoons extra-virgin olive oil

2 tablespoons butter

2 tablespoons balsamic vinegar

½ cup chicken broth, either homemade or canned low-sodium

½ tablespoon dried oregano

3 tablespoons chopped fresh Italian parsley

¼ cup freshly grated Parmigiano-Reggiano cheese

On your mark . . .

- Wash the chicken pieces and remove as much of the fat and skin as you can.

- Dry the chicken very well with paper towels to prevent spattering when you brown it.

- In a small bowl, mix the flour with 2 teaspoons of the salt and pepper to taste.

- Roll a piece of the chicken in the flour mixture. Then shake off any excess flour and place the piece on a platter.

- Repeat until all the chicken is floured. Set aside. Wash the cutting board and knives that were used with the raw chicken.

Get set . . .

- Peel and thinly slice the onion.

- Wash and chop the carrot.

- Peel and finely chop the garlic.

- If the mushrooms have a lot of dirt on them, carefully brush them clean with a paper towel. Then cut them into quarters.

- Drain the tomatoes in a hand strainer.

Cook!

- Place a 12-inch skillet over medium heat and add the olive oil and butter.

- After the butter has melted and the foam disappears, brown the

chicken pieces, a few at a time, on both sides, starting with the largest pieces first. It will take about 10 to 15 minutes to brown all the chicken.

- As the pieces brown, place them on a clean platter. Do not return the browned chicken to the platter that held the raw pieces.

- After the browning is complete, have an adult assistant help you pour out all the fat in the skillet except 1 tablespoon.

- Reheat the skillet on medium heat. Add the onion and cook for 3 to 4 minutes.

- Add the balsamic vinegar, bring to a boil, and cook for about 30 seconds.

- Add the carrot, garlic, mushrooms, tomatoes, chicken broth, oregano, and the remaining 1 ½ teaspoons of salt. Stir well and cook for 1 minute.

- Return the chicken to the skillet, spooning some sauce over each piece, and bring to a soft boil.

- Cover the pan with a tight-fitting lid and reduce the heat to simmer. Cook for 40 to 50 minutes, or until the chicken is very tender.

- To serve, spoon the sauce over the chicken, sprinkle the chopped parsley and grated cheese over the top, and bring to the table.

Country-Style Pork
Spezzatino di Maiale

In the south of Italy, between the sole and heel of the Italian boot, is a sunbathed, ancient region called Basilicata. Here is an adaptation of a classic recipe from the town of Matera. The pork is baked in the oven in a heavy pot. Italian chefs like to use an enameled or cast-iron pot, but any heavy pot will work.

Serves 6

Ingredients

2 ½ pounds center cut boneless pork loin

2 medium-size russet or Yukon gold potatoes

1 medium-size onion

3 cloves garlic

½ cup chopped fresh or canned tomatoes

½ teaspoon dried oregano or ½ tablespoon fresh

1 teaspoon dried rosemary or ½ tablespoon fresh

5 or 6 fresh basil leaves, torn into small pieces, or 1 teaspoon dried basil

2 teaspoons salt

¼ teaspoon crushed red pepper (optional)

¼ cup extra-virgin olive oil

fresh Italian parsley for garnish

On your mark, get set . . .

- Preheat the oven to 375°F.

- Cut the pork loin into 1- to 1 ½-inch cubes. Try to keep the cubes all about the same size so that they will cook evenly.

- Place the pork cubes in a heavy ovenproof pot and set aside. Wash the cutting board that you used for the pork.

- Rinse and scrub the potatoes, making sure to remove all the dirt.

- Leaving the skins on, cut the potatoes in half lengthwise. Cut each half into long slices, then cut the slices into 1-inch cubes. Add the potatoes to the pork.

- Peel and chop the onion, measure ¾ cup, and add to the pork.

- Peel and chop the garlic and add to the pork.

- Next add the chopped tomatoes, oregano, rosemary, basil, salt, and crushed red pepper.

- Pour the olive oil over all the ingredients and carefully toss everything together with a large spoon.

Cook!

- Cover the pot and place on the middle rack of the oven.

- Bake for 1 hour. About halfway through the baking, use hot pads to carefully lift the lid, and stir the pot with a large spoon. Try to coat all the ingredients with sauce.

- After another 30 minutes, check to see if the pork and potatoes are tender. If they are, the dish is ready to serve. If the pork is not yet tender, bake for another 10 to 15 minutes.

- Spoon some of the sauce over the top, garnish with parsley, and serve hot.

Asparagus with Parmesan and Butter
Asparagi alla Parmigiana

Do you know what makes asparagus such a delicacy? One asparagus plant takes three years to mature before it is ready to be picked. Asparagus is grown in many parts of Italy, but no matter where it comes from, it is a treat. The baskets of fresh asparagus that begin to appear in the markets of the Emilia-Romagna region create lots of excitement, not only for their taste but also because they are a sure sign that spring has arrived. The wild asparagus from the Roman countryside is prized for its flavor, as is the white asparagus from the area around Venice. The following classic recipe from the city of Parma combines this wonderful vegetable with the famous Parmigiano-Reggiano cheese.

Serves 6

Ingredients

2 pounds fresh asparagus

2 cups water

2 tablespoons salt

2 tablespoons butter

2 tablespoons extra-virgin olive oil

⅔ cup freshly grated Parmigiano-Reggiano cheese

On your mark, get set . . .

- Rinse the asparagus with cold water.

- Take 1 stalk at a time in both hands and snap off the bottom. The stalk will naturally break at the place where it is most tender. Discard the tougher bottom part and drop the upper part into a bowl of cold water.

- Repeat with all the stalks. If the asparagus you are using is very fresh and thin, you need only snap off about 1 inch from the bottom of the stalk.

Cook!

- Preheat the oven to 425°F.

- In a pan that is large enough to hold all the asparagus, bring 2 cups water to a boil. Add the salt.

- Add the asparagus and cover the pan. As soon as the water boils again, remove the cover, reduce the heat to low, and cook for 4 to 5 minutes.

- Using tongs, remove 1 stalk and test for doneness. If you like your asparagus crisp, it should be done. If you like your asparagus more tender, let it cook for another 3 to 4 minutes. To stop the cooking, run cold water over the asparagus.

- Place the cooked asparagus in the bottom of a baking pan just large enough to hold it all.

- Heat the butter and olive oil in a small saucepan over low heat.

- When the butter is melted, pour over the asparagus and toss well to cover. Top with the grated cheese.

- Bake for 10 minutes, or until a golden crusty top covers the asparagus.

- Serve hot on a platter.

Chef's Tip

Asparagus is best cooked the day you buy (or pick) it. It will stay fresh in the refrigerator for up to four days, but you must wrap it well.

Green Beans with Tomatoes, Roman Style
Fagiolini alla Romana

The people of Rome are surrounded by some of the most beautiful landscapes in Italy. The farmers grow outstanding vegetables and the cooks of Rome know just what to do with them. Try this dish and you will know why vegetables are such an important part of Italian cooking. Enjoy it hot, or make it a day ahead and serve it cold as a salad.

Serves 6

Ingredients

1 ½ pounds fresh green beans

1 cup canned chopped tomatoes

1 small onion

1 clove garlic

1 tablespoon extra-virgin olive oil

1 tablespoon butter

2 teaspoons salt

2 or 3 sprigs fresh Italian parsley, chopped

On your mark, get set . . .

- Wash the green beans, snap in half, and drop into a bowl of cold water.
- Pour the tomatoes into a hand strainer to drain. Discard the tomato juice.
- Peel and chop the onion.
- Peel and chop the garlic.

Cook!

- Place a 10-inch skillet over medium-low heat and add the olive oil and butter.
- When the butter and oil start to bubble, add the onion and garlic. Cook slowly for 4 to 5 minutes, or until they are golden in color.
- Add the tomatoes and bring to a slight boil.
- Drain the green beans through a colander, then add them to the

skillet, along with the salt. Carefully toss the beans with the tomatoes.

- Cover the pan, reduce the heat to simmer, and cook for 30 minutes, or until the beans are tender. Halfway through the cooking, raise the lid and check to see if the liquid has cooked away. If it has, add a few tablespoons of cold water.

- When ready to serve, add the chopped parsley and bring to the table in a serving bowl.

Desserts

Chocolate and
walnut cake.

Chocolate and Walnut Cake
Torta al Cioccolato con Noci

The Italian soil produces many treasures and walnuts are certainly one of them. Here is a recipe inspired by a classic from the Liguria region of northern Italy. This dessert combines the Italians' love of chocolate and walnuts to create a dense cake that is almost flourless. Serve it with vanilla ice cream or whipped cream and watch it disappear.

Serves 6 to 8

Ingredients

2 tablespoons plus 1 teaspoon butter

3 teaspoons plain bread crumbs

1 cup chopped walnuts

8 to 10 ounces milk chocolate with almonds

1 ⅔ cups confectioners' sugar plus 1 tablespoon for decorating

1 tablespoon all-purpose flour

¼ teaspoon ground cinnamon

4 eggs

1 teaspoon pure vanilla extract

1 tablespoon orange juice

vanilla ice cream or whipped cream for serving

On your mark . . .

- Preheat the oven to 350°F.

- Grease a 9 ½-inch round cake pan with 1 teaspoon of the butter.

- Sprinkle the bread crumbs over the bottom of the pan.

- Tip the pan and slowly rotate in a circle, allowing the bread crumbs to evenly cover the entire surface of the pan, sides and bottom. Carefully tap out any excess bread crumbs and discard. Set the pan aside.

- Melt the remaining 2 tablespoons of butter in a small saucepan over low heat.

- Set aside.

Get set . . .

- Pour the chopped walnuts onto a sheet of wax paper.

- Using a rolling pin, crush the walnuts into a coarse powder, but don't overdo it. You still want chunks of walnut left.

- Empty the walnuts into a bowl.
- Chop the chocolate into small pieces and add to the walnuts.
- Add 1 ⅓ cups of the confectioners' sugar.
- Add the flour and cinnamon and mix well.
- Break the eggs into a separate bowl and add the vanilla and orange juice. Beat the eggs on high speed for about 30 seconds, using an electric hand mixer.
- Add the walnut-chocolate mixture to the eggs and stir with a rubber spatula or wooden spoon until just combined.
- Add the melted butter and give the batter a few more stirs. Do not overmix.

Cook!

- Pour the batter into the cake pan and bake on the middle rack of the oven for 50 to 55 minutes. The cake is done when the middle is firm to the touch and the sides have just begun to pull away from the pan. (After it is baked, the cake will settle to about 1 inch thick.)

- Remove the cake from the oven and place on a rack. Let cool for 10 minutes.

- Run a knife around the edge to loosen it from the sides. Place a dish that is larger than the pan on top. Using hot pads, if you need them, turn the cake pan and the dish upside down. The cake should slip down onto the dish.

- Place the cooling rack on top of the cake and turn the cake over again. Now let it cool completely.

- To decorate, place the remaining 1 tablespoon of confectioners' sugar in a hand strainer. Lightly tap the strainer over the cake and let the sugar snow across the top. Or use a shaker and lightly sprinkle the cake with the confectioners' sugar.

- Serve with vanilla ice cream or whipped cream.

Fresh Fruit with Strawberry Glaze
Macedonia con Glassa alle Fragole

Fresh fruits are a very popular part of any Italian meal, so it's no surprise that this famous dessert is loved all over Italy. In choosing fruits for this dish, look for those that are ripe and flavorful, but not too soft. In the summer there is nothing like cold fruit on a hot day. Also, there is nothing like fresh fruit in the fall or winter to remind us of those summer days. Either way, no matter what the season, this is a great dessert.

Serves 6

Ingredients

1 cup freshly squeezed orange juice

¼ cup freshly squeezed lemon juice

2 pears

2 apples

2 bananas

4 cups other fresh fruit, such as plums, melon, tangerines, grapefruit, kiwis, peaches, seedless grapes, blueberries, raspberries, or pitted cherries

GLAZE

½ cup strawberry jam

2 tablespoons freshly squeezed orange juice

On your mark, get set . . .

- Pour 1 cup orange juice into a large bowl. Add the lemon juice.
- Peel the pears and apples, remove the seeds, and cut into chunks. Add them to the bowl.
- Peel and slice the bananas and add to the bowl.
- Wash and prepare the rest of the fruit, removing the skins and seeds where necessary, and measure out 4 cups. Add to the bowl.

Toss!

- Gently toss the fruit, making sure all the pieces are coated with the juices.

- For the glaze, combine the strawberry jam with 2 tablespoons of orange juice. Pour over the fruit and toss again until all the fruit is lightly glazed.

- Chill for 1 to 4 hours, but not overnight or the fruit will get soggy. Serve cold.

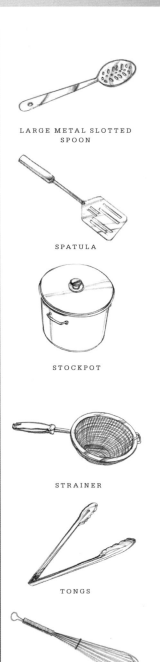

Helpful Kitchen Equipment and Utensils

BAKING PAN

BREAD PAN

COLANDER

COOKIE SHEETS

CUTTING BOARD

ELECTRIC HAND MIXER

FOOD PROCESSOR

FOUR-SIDED GRATER

KNIVES, ASSORTED

LADLE

MEASURING CUPS

MEASURING SPOONS

MIXING BOWLS, ASSORTED

PIZZA PAN

ROLLING PIN

SALAD SPINNER

SAUCEPANS WITH LIDS, ASSORTED SIZES

SKILLETS

LARGE METAL SLOTTED SPOON

SPATULA

STOCKPOT

STRAINER

TONGS

WHISK

Anchovies

This tiny fish packs a large punch of flavor. Anchovies are a very misunderstood ingredient in the Italian kitchen and, unfortunately, often get a negative response from people who are afraid to try them. When shopping, look for the anchovies in glass jars rather than cans. They are larger and have better flavor. Rinse and pat the anchovies dry before you use them. If you have any anchovies left over, pack them back in the glass jar, cover with extra-virgin olive oil, and refrigerate.

Arborio Rice

Arborio is one of nearly fifty varieties of rice grown in Italy. The grain is short and fat with a pearl white exterior and has a high starch content. Arborio is less processed in the mill than other rice and cooking releases the starch giving the rice a creamy texture with a slight crunchy interior.

Balsamic Vinegar

See Vinegar

Basil

Look for fresh basil that is bright green and has no dark spots. Use only the leaves of this herb, not the stems. There are many varieties of basil to choose from, even red. Red basil is called opal, and it will work as well as green with all the recipes in this book. Basil leaves can hold dirt. Wash them well, then pat the leaves dry. The best way to use basil is not to cut it with a knife. Tear it with your fingers and you will not bruise it.

Bread Crumbs

The best bread crumbs are the ones you make yourself. Old bread that has hardened makes really good crumbs. Grate it with a hand grater, using the tiniest holes. Be careful not to grate your knuckles along with the bread. You can also buy bread crumbs. Look for the ones marked "plain." They will have no salt or extra seasoning. That way you can season them yourself.

Broth or Stock

There is nothing quite as delicious as homemade broth to add flavor to a dish. Broth is the liquid in which chicken, meat, fish, or vegetables have been cooked; when that liquid is used as the base for soup or a sauce, it is called stock. Follow the recipe in this book to make your own broth. If you buy canned broth, look for "low-sodium" on the label.

Capers

These are buds or blooms from a Mediterranean shrub that have been preserved and packed in vinegar or salt water. The ones packed in salt water generally taste better. No matter which ones you get, you must rinse them several times before you use them. Look for the larger-size capers rather than the small ones; they will have more flavor.

Fontina Cheese

This is a semisoft cheese with a buttery and nutty flavor. The best comes from the northern Alpine region of Italy. If you can't find Italian fontina, you can use Danish fontina instead.

Garlic

Garlic is a member of the onion family and is a valuable flavor maker in Italian cooking. When you purchase garlic, look for large bulbs that are hard and solid. Inside the bulb are cloves. To use the cloves, first separate them from the bulb. With the flat side of a knife, give them a good whack, then remove the white paper-thin skin and cut off the dark tip. The cloves can be chopped into small pieces, mashed, or cut into thin slices. A garlic press is a great way to extract flavor from the cloves. Many nutritionists believe that garlic has great health benefits because it is rich in minerals. The world is separated into two groups of people: those who love garlic and those who don't. Which are you?

Mozzarella Cheese

A delicate white cheese made from cow's or buffalo's milk, mozzarella melts wonderfully and is an important ingredient in many Italian dishes. It is available in Italian specialty markets or cheese stores. You can also purchase mozzarella at almost any supermarket. If you buy it fresh, use it the same day or no later than the next day. If you buy it packaged, be sure to check the expiration date.

Nutmeg

This spice is native to Indonesia. The Venetians and the cooks of Bologna love cooking with nutmeg. If used in moderation, it gives dishes a warm, soft flavor. But be careful! Nutmeg can be an overpowering flavor, so don't overdo it. It is best to buy it whole and grate only what you need for your recipe. Store the nutmeg sealed in a glass jar and it will keep for a long time.

Olive Oil

There are many varieties and grades of olive oil. Olive oil is called "extra-virgin" if it has been obtained from the first pressing of the olives without the use of chemicals and has low acidity (less than 1 percent). It also has great flavor. Cold pressed extra-virgin olive oil is regarded as the best of the extra-virgin olive oils. "Cold pressed" means that the olives were pressed without heat, so the oil keeps lots of flavor. The flavor of good olive oil will enhance any salad dressing you make. Extra-virgin oil can be expensive, however, so consider your budget when buying it. Store olive oil away from bright sunlight, in cool temperatures.

Oregano

Dried or fresh, this pungent herb is full of flavor. It is perfect for pizza, tomato sauces, chicken dishes, and vegetables. Be careful not to overdo it. Too much oregano can overpower a dish. Used sparingly, it is an essential part of the flavor of Italian cooking. Dried oregano, stored in a covered glass jar, will keep for about six months.

Parmesan

This hard grating cheese made from cow's milk is named after the region where it originated, Parma. Domestic Parmesan, widely available in stores, is usually sold already grated and is generally blended with preservatives to ensure a long shelf life. It is popular and affordable, but it hardly compares with the flavor or delicacy of imported Parmesan. It is best to buy Parmesan in a wedge and grate it as you need it to keep it at peak flavor. To store, wrap in wax paper and then aluminum foil and keep in the coldest part of the refrigerator.

Parmigiano-Reggiano

This golden cheese is so famous in Italy that it has its own set of laws to regulate how it should be made. Once you taste it, you will know why it is called the "king of Italian cheese." Parmigiano-Reggiano has been made for over five hundred years, but the official recipe used today in Parma and Reggio Emilia was only established in 1955. It is lower in fat and cholesterol than many other cheeses. You can recognize it easily because its name is always stamped into the rind of the cheese. It is best to buy it in a wedge and grate it as you need it to keep it at peak flavor. To store, wrap in wax paper and then aluminum foil and keep in the coldest part of the refrigerator. Parmigiano-Reggiano is expensive, so consider your budget when shopping for it. You may substitute Parmesan cheese, but try not to buy it already grated.

Parsley, Fresh Italian Flat-Leaf

This variety of parsley is full of flavor. Look for bright green leaves and stems that are not wilted or shriveled. Be sure you don't make a common mistake and buy coriander, a similar-looking herb. Wash the parsley before you use it and chop it, using both the stems and the leaves to get the best flavor.

Pepper, Whole Black

There is a real difference in the flavor of black pepper when it is freshly ground. You are probably most familiar with the ground pepper that you buy in the store. Chances are it was ground months earlier and the flavor has diminished. Grinding your own peppercorns requires a pepper mill. Use pepper with caution because it can overpower the flavor of a dish and make it very hot.

Radicchio

This plant is a member of the chicory family. A head of radicchio is just a little larger than an orange and has delicate red and white lettuce-like leaves. Radicchio makes a great addition to any salad. Look for firm, solid heads with no wilted or brown leaves. Wash the leaves and pat them dry with paper towels or dry in a salad spinner. Belgian endive is a good substitute.

Tomatoes

There is no doubt that tomatoes are the key ingredient in a lot of Italian cooking. When shopping for fresh tomatoes, look for rich, red color and avoid the fruits with spots or bruises. If you are unable to find good fresh tomatoes, don't hesitate to buy canned. To store fresh tomatoes, keep them away from heat, but never put them in the refrigerator. The cold will destroy their flavor and texture.

Vinegar

Balsamic vinegar is from the Emilia-Romagna region in northern Italy. Balsamic has been made in this region for over a thousand years. There are many grades of balsamic vinegar and prices can range from inexpensive to very costly. The price and quality are determined by the age of the vinegar and where it originated. Inexpensive balsamic will work quite well for the recipes in this book.

Red wine vinegar is very popular in salad dressings in Italy. It has a deep, rich flavor. Look for red wine vinegar that is bright red and not cloudy.

Books

Bisignano, Alphonse. *Cooking the Italian Way*. Minneapolis, MN: Lerner Publishing Group, 2001.

Gioffre, Rosalba. *Fun with Italian Cooking*. New York: Powerkids Press, 2009.

Kras, Sara Louise. *The Food of Italy* (Flavors of the World). Tarrytown, NY: Marshall Cavendish Benchmark Books, 2012.

Websites

Italian History

www.kidspast.com/world-history/0289-the-renaissance-italy.php
The Renaissance section of this site allows the student to browse through Italian history, with a detour to the English Renaissance. Colorful pictures and interesting text make it easy to learn about this important period.

Visual Geography Series

http://vgsbooks.com/
To access this site's information about the land of Italy, its government, cultural life, and economy, just select "Italy" from the list of links on the left.

Metric Conversion Chart

You can use the chart below to convert from U.S. measurements to the metric system.

Weight
1 ounce = 28 grams
½ pound (8 ounces) = 227 grams
1 pound = .45 kilogram
2.2 pounds = 1 kilogram

Liquid volume
1 teaspoon = 5 milliliters
1 tablespoon = 15 milliliters
1 fluid ounce = 30 milliliters
1 cup = 240 milliliters (.24 liter)
1 pint = 480 milliliters (.48 liter)
1 quart = .95 liter

Length
¼ inch = .6 centimeter
½ inch = 1.25 centimeters
1 inch = 2.5 centimeters

Temperature
100°F = 40°C
110°F = 45°C
212°F = 100°C (boiling point of water)
350°F = 180°C
375°F = 190°C
400°F = 200°C
425°F = 220°C
450°F = 235°C

(To convert temperatures in Fahrenheit to Celsius, subtract 32 and multiply by .56)

Page numbers in **boldface** are photographs.

About the Author

Chef Matthew Locricchio knows a thing or two about cooking. What sets this chef apart from other talented professionals in his field is his knack for imparting this culinary wisdom to children. Matthew was born in Michigan and into a restaurant and catering family, and has spent most of his life in the food industry. Along with his years of training as a chef and his numerous books on cooking, Matthew has made guest appearances on Martha Stewart Radio, *Everyday Food* to talk about his unique approach to getting kids interested in cooking. He has also been heard on *The Faith Middleton Show: Food Schmooze*, on National Public Radio (NPR), and seen on WGN TV, *Lunch Break*, in Chicago.

Matthew's award-winning *The 2nd International Cookbook for Kids* followed up on his earlier *The International Cookbook for Kids*, and, much like the first book, is full of delicious, kid-friendly recipes from around the world.

Also a playwright and actor, Matthew has worked in numerous commercials, soap operas, films, and television shows. Chef Locricchio has been a guest instructor at The Institute of Culinary Education in New York City and Stonewall Kitchen in York, Maine. He guest lectures in the series "Adventures in the Global Kitchen for Kids and Families" at The American Museum of Natural History in New York City.

His brand new *Teen Cuisine*, with spectacular photos by James Beard Winner, James Peterson, was released October 1, 2010. He is currently writing a follow-up with a vegetarian cookbook.

More information about Matthew Locricchio can be found at his website: www.cookbooksandkids.com or www.teencuisinebooks.com